First World War
and Army of Occupation
War Diary
France, Belgium and Germany

66 DIVISION
199 Infantry Brigade
Manchester Regiment
2/8th Battalion
1 September 1915 - 10 February 1916

WO95/3145/3

The Naval & Military Press Ltd
www.nmarchive.com
Published in association with The National Archives

Published by

The Naval & Military Press Ltd

Unit 10 Ridgewood Industrial Park,

Uckfield, East Sussex,

TN22 5QE England

Tel: +44 (0) 1825 749494

www.naval-military-press.com

www.nmarchive.com

This diary has been reprinted in facsimile from the original. Any imperfections are inevitably reproduced and the quality may fall short of modern type and cartographic standards.

© Crown Copyright
Images reproduced by permission of The National Archives, London, England, 2015.

Contents

Document type	Place/Title	Date From	Date To
Heading	WO95/3145/3 2/8 Battalion Manchester Reg		
Heading	66 Div 199 Bde 2/8 Bn. Manchester Regt. 1915 Sep-1916 Feb		
War Diary	Crowborough	01/09/1915	10/09/1915
War Diary	Burham	18/09/1915	20/09/1915
War Diary	Crowborough	21/09/1915	25/09/1915
Miscellaneous	Statement In Accordance With Central Force Circular Memo Number 468 Dated 20th September 1914	03/09/1915	03/09/1915
War Diary	Crowborough	04/10/1915	10/02/1916
War Diary	Hartfield	02/02/1916	02/02/1916
War Diary	Crowborough	05/02/1916	10/02/1916

WO/95/3145/3

218 Battalion Machete Reg.

66 DIV

199 BDE

2/8 BN. MANCHESTER REGT.

1915 SEP — 1916 FEB

3032

Army Form C. 2118.

WAR DIARY
—or—
INTELLIGENCE SUMMARY
(Erase heading not required.)

Instructions regarding War Diaries and Intelligence Summaries are contained in F.S. Regs., Part II. and the Staff Manual respectively. Title pages will be prepared in manuscript.

Hour, Date, Place	Summary of Events and Information	Remarks and references to Appendices
1915.		
Sept.1st. Crowborough.		
" 9th "	2 Sets Pack Saddlery received.	
" 10th "	11 Sets heavy pole draught harness received.	
" 18th Burham.	1 Maltese Cart received.	
" 19/20th "	2nd Lieut. J.G.Evans joined for duty.	
	March from Burham to Crowborough, halting at Tonbridge on night of 19/20th September.	
" 21st Crowborough.	Signalling Stores, 4 buzzers and 2 electric field lamps received.	
" 22nd "	4 L.D. mules received from A.S.C.	
" 24th "	2 Riding Horses received from A.S.C.	
" 25th "	4 Travelling Kitchens received.	
Sept.30th/Oct.1st "	Brigade Outpost Scheme including bivouac on night of Sept.30th/Oct. 1st.	

.... Lieut.Colonel.
Comdg. 2/8th Bn.Manchester Regt.

STATEMENT IN ACCORDANCE WITH CENTRAL FORCE CIRCULAR
MEMO NUMBER 468 DATED 20TH SEPTEMBER 1914.

UNIT..2/8th Battalion Manchester Regt.
BRIGADE...................................199th Infantry Brigade.
DIVISION...................................66th (East Lancashire) Division.
MOBILIZATION CENTRE............Manchester.
TEMPORARY WAR STATION........Burham Camp, Eccles, Nr. Maidstone.
STATIONS SINCE OCCUPIED
SUBSEQUENT TO CONCENTRATION....Southport - Crowborough - Burham.

(a) MOBILISATION....................... *Nil*

(b) CONCENTRATION AT WAR STATIONS.
(Including railway moves)........

(c) ORGANIZATION FOR DEFENCE.
(Including vulnerable points)....

(d) TRAINING............................. *Progressive*

(e) DISCIPLINE........................... *The general conduct of the men is good*

(f) ADMINISTRATION.....................

    (1) Medical Services.......... *A Medical Officer is still required*

    (2) Veterinary Services....... *No Remarks*

    (3) Supply Services........... *Satisfactory*

    (4) Transport Services....... *Improving but there are still deficiencies, especially in vehicles*

    (5) Ordnance Services........ *Satisfactory*

    (6) Billeting and Hutting.... *Huts in good condition*

    (7) Channels of correspondence
        in routine matters........

    (8) Range Construction........ *Nil*

    (9) Supply of Remounts........ *Improved*

(g) REORGANISATION OF T.F. INTO
HOME & IMPERIAL SERVICE........... *No change*

(h) PREPARATION OF UNITS FOR
IMPERIAL SERVICE.................. *No change*

A.H. Crosland
Lieut. Colonel,
Commanding 2/8th Bn.
Manchester Regiment.

Burham Camp
3/9/15.

Army Form C. 2118.

WAR DIARY
or
INTELLIGENCE SUMMARY.
(Erase heading not required.)

Instructions regarding War Diaries and Intelligence Summaries are contained in F.S. Regs., Part II. and the Staff Manual respectively. Title pages will be prepared in manuscript.

199/86

Hour, Date, Place	Summary of Events and Information	Remarks and references to Appendices
4th Oct.1915. Crowborough.	Three Officers embarked for Foreign Service as reinforcements to 1/8th Bn Manchester Regiment.	
14th Oct,1915. -do-	One Wagon civilian pattern received from A.S.C.	
17th Oct,1915. -do-	Five L.D. Horses received from A.S.C.	
21st Oct,1915. -do-	Four limbered Wagons and three Riding Horses received from A.S.C.	
29th Oct,1915. -do-	66 .256 Rifles and 19800 rounds of ammunition sent to 83rd Provisional Battn, Burnham-on-Crouch.	
29th Oct,1915. -do-	9 .256 Rifles and 2700 rounds of Ammunition sent to 28th Provisional Battalion, Southend.	

Crowborough.
3/11/15.

J.H.Frostand
Lieut. Colonel.
Comdg. 2/8th Bn Manchester Regt.

2/8th Bn. Manchester Regiment.
WAR DIARY

Army Form C. 2118.
Crowborough.
3/12/15.

INTELLIGENCE SUMMARY.
(Erase heading not required.)

Instructions regarding War Diaries and Intelligence Summaries are contained in F.S. Regs., Part II. and the Staff Manual respectively. Title pages will be prepared in manuscript.

Hour, Date, Place	Summary of Events and Information	Remarks and references to Appendices
19th Nov.1915, Crowborough.	Inspection by Major General E.T. Dickson. An Outpost Scheme was carried out. The General commented on the absence of written Orders. These are now issued in all Field Operations carried out by this Unit.	
22nd Nov.1915, Crowborough.	All Japanese Rifles (525 in number), bayonets, and ammunition in possession returned to Weedon, and .303 Charger Loading M.L.E. Rifles (540 in number) with bayonets, and .303 ammunition, received in exchange.	

.... Lieut. Colonel.
Comdg. 2/8th Bn. Manchester Regt.

2/8th Bn. Manchester Regt.

WAR DIARY
or
INTELLIGENCE SUMMARY.
(*Erase heading not required.*)

Army Form C. 2118.

Instructions regarding War Diaries and Intelligence Summaries are contained in F.S. Regs., Part II and the Staff Manual respectively. Title pages will be prepared in manuscript.

Hour, Date, Place	Summary of Events and Information	Remarks and references to Appendices
10:30 a.m. Dec. 11th 1915. Crowborough.	Inspection by G.O.C. 66th (East Lancashire) Division.	Ans.
10:30 a.m. Dec. 14th 1915. do	Inspection of the Battalion in Physical Training & Bayonet Fighting by Assistant Inspector of Gymnasia.	Ans.

.... Lieut.-Colonel.
Comdg. 2/8th Bn. Manchester Regiment.

Army Form C. 2118.

WAR DIARY
or
INTELLIGENCE SUMMARY.
(Erase heading not required.)

Instructions regarding War Diaries and Intelligence Summaries are contained in F.S. Regs., Part II. and the Staff Manual respectively. Title pages will be prepared in manuscript.

199/66

Hour, Date, Place	Summary of Events and Information	Remarks and references to Appendices
22/1/16. Crowborough.	First batch of "Derby" recruits (11 in number) received.	
25/1/16. -do-	Second " " " (10 in number) received.	
29/1/16. -do-	Third " " " (19 in number) received.	

Crowborough, Sussex.
3rd February, 1916.

F.A. Harrock, Major.
for Lieut. Colonel.
Comdg. 2/8th Bn Manchester Regt.

Army Form C. 2118.

WAR DIARY
or
INTELLIGENCE SUMMARY.
(Erase heading not required.)

Instructions regarding War Diaries and Intelligence Summaries are contained in F.S. Regs., Part II. and the Staff Manual respectively. Title pages will be prepared in manuscript.

Hour, Date, Place			Summary of Events and Information	Remarks and references to Appendices
2 p.m.	1/2/16	CROYBOROUGH	Fourth batch of "DERBY" recruits (10 in number) received	ymg
	2/2/16	HARTFIELD	Inspection of 1st Line Transport by G.O.C. 66th (2nd Division)	ymg
5/2/16		CROWBOROUGH	Fifth batch of "DERBY" recruits (19 in number) received.	ymg
	8/2/16	do	do " " (24 in number) received	ymg
10.30 a.m.	10/2/16	do	Inspection of Battalion and Helmets by O.C. 199th Infantry Brigade	ymg
2 p.m.	10/2/16	do	Inspection of Battalion in Physical Training and Bayonet fighting by Assistant Superintendent of Gymnasia, C.H. & C.C.	ymg

R.W. Rutland
Lt. Colonel.
2/8th Bn. Manchester Regt.

www.ingramcontent.com/pod-product-compliance
Lightning Source LLC
Chambersburg PA
CBHW081518160426
43193CB00014B/2724